God bless you!
Gary St... 
Ps 45:1

# Dedication

To those who have gone before,
those who walk alongside,
and those who will follow.

*My heart is stirred by a noble theme as I recite my verses for the king.*
—Psalm 45:1

ISBN 13: 978-1-60615-019-1
ISBN 10: 1-60615-019-7
Library of Congress Catalog Card Number: 2009933049

Printed in China.

# Contents

# Introduction

*Faith is being sure of what we hope for and certain of what we do not see . . . without faith it is impossible to please God, because anyone who comes to him must believe that he exists and that he rewards those who earnestly seek him.*

—Hebrews 11:1, 6

I had no hope for the future when the dream described in poem #2, "Beyond a Dream," occurred. But God says in his Word, "I know the plans I have for you . . . plans to give you hope and a future" (Jer. 29:11). This collection exists because of God's grace and his work of faith in my life.

I believed God existed and that he created the earth and everything in it. Nothing so beautiful and intricately detailed as the universe could just "happen" or evolve over time. Romans 1:19–20 (MSG) puts it this way: "The basic reality of God is plain enough. Open your eyes and there it is! By taking a long and thoughtful look at what God has created, people have always been able to see what their eyes as such can't see . . ." I'd regularly attended church for as long as I could remember, but I did not yet see that I could have a living relationship with this Creator-God.

A series of serious health issues from birth, plus chronic anxiety and depression, made life difficult. I couldn't believe God would allow such things to happen. Life should have meaning and purpose, not what I experienced. After my dream, my goal became to find God. I discovered he was more than eager for me to find him. God wants more than religion; he wants relationship through faith in Jesus Christ, who gave his life for that very purpose. John 3:16 says, "God so loved the world that he gave his only Son, Jesus Christ, so that whosoever believes in him would have eternal life."

When we respond to God, our lives are changed forever. God's unique purpose for our lives will follow as we follow him. Jesus asks each one of us: "Will you follow me?" My sincere desire is that this book will lead you to the Savior and you will respond to his call on your life.

Wheaton College Campus, Wheaton, Illinois

# Be Still

Lord, if I sit here quietly,
will you find me?

Maybe it's easier to find you.

Dawn over Gulf of Mexico

# Beyond a Dream

Night of the world,
darkness so profound
it seemed an endless well.
No light, no sound,
forever dropping down,
world without end.

Then quite persistently,
a gentle bend
and turning up
I find I'm not alone,
have never been.

The One who kept the walls
from caving in above
is now beneath,
supporting, holding up.

Comes the dawn,
filling all the universe
with light

and there am I, a tiny child
curled up in the lap of God;
the One who followed all along.

San Juan City Hall—San Juan, Puerto Rico

# Circular Thought

Jehovah "I AM"
who was and is,
and will always be,
unchanged for all eternity.
Alpha, Omega,
beginning and end
creator, sustainer
servant-friend.
Comforter, teacher
Shepherd. Amen.
God Almighty
with Jesus his Son
and Holy Spirit,
three in one.

Uncreated,
God was born
then died, went to hell,
and rose Easter morn.

Before time began
God had a plan
to prove forever
he is "I AM."

Mount Sinai, Jabil Musa, Sinai Peninsula

# Climbing Mount Sinai

They seem so small,
just tiny dots of light
climbing up the mountain.
So far away
one hardly seems
to make a difference at all
in the vast eternity of space
and all of time.

But one, by one, by one
they climb to the heights
and far beyond,
they shine like stars.
Stretching down
they guide my feet
and fill my soul
with God's celestial light.

I am one,
just one . . . but one
small beam to those below,
one reflection of a greater Son,
one witness to eternal light;
one more difference in the night.

Montezuma National Wildlife Refuge, New York

# Cloak of Gentleness

Teach me to be gentle, Lord, to put away all pettiness and pride.

Teach me by your gentle Word
to lay all bitterness aside.

And teach me, gentle Lord,
in your grace to abide.

Wheaton College Campus, Wheaton, Illinois

# Commission

Christ charges us
to be pinpoints of light
in a universe of darkness.
Fireflies in the night
for a darkened world to see.

Shoreline—Cayuga Lake, New York

# Connection

Teach me, Lord, to sit
in silence and see your open heart . . .
then rise and obey.

Site of Jacob's well—Nablus, Israel

# Cross Purpose

Truth be told,
Jesus had to die on Calvary.
No other way
would get God's point across.

God's personal touch
was to give his only Son.
How else could we find
Jesus here, today,
across all of time?

Heaven's loss was our gain.
God loves each of us that much.

Honestly!

Glorieta Conference Center—Santé Fe, New Mexico

# Faith Lifts

Faith sees my Savior on the cross,
humbly accepts God's grace.
Faith stirs my heart and voice to praise,
lifts Christ to his rightful place.

Faith lifts me up; Jesus sets me free.
Faith walks through the valley and the fire,
beckons me to walk upon the sea.
Faith races toward my wildest dreams,
Past the obstacles I see.

Faith lifts me up, sees God's plan for me.
Faith holds my hand when my flesh is weak
and considers every battle won.
Faith lifts me up to stand on solid ground,
confidently living in God's Son.

Faith lifts me up to more than I can be.

Sight and Sound Millennium Theater—Lancaster, Pennsylvania

20

# Faith that Stands

Lord, when I don't understand
I'll hold your hand;
I know you are near.

If answers don't come,
I won't succumb to doubt and fear.

Your grace saved my life,
canceled all my strife,
and you've made it clear
no matter what life holds
my faith stands strong and bold
when you are here.

Butterfly farm—St. Maartan

# Faith to Faith

Faith takes a solid stand
sight could not confirm.

Faith makes a quantum leap
hesitance would spurn.

Faith knows God hears the prayer
reason can't believe,

Faith holds out forgiveness
pride cannot conceive.

Faith stands steady in the fire
fear could never face.

Faith walks upon the water,
doubt sinks without a trace.

Faith stretches out a hand,
indifference withholds,

Faith speaks the Word of God
while apathy turns cold.

Faith endures until the end
and steps from grace to grace,

Faith stands whole before his throne
and sees God face to face.

Atlantic Ocean—Caribbean

# Genesis Hymn

My mind cannot conceive the birth of life
nor fathom how the ocean depths were formed;
or grasp a star-decked universe at night,
the heavens and the earth so God-adorned.

My soul can only soar to heights unknown
in adoration of my Lord and King.
My spirit sings for joy and shouts his praise,
my life, my breath, my song, my everything!

Butterfly farm—St. Maartan

# Hallelujah!

Gossamer wings lift
silent praises to heaven.

A butterfly sings!

Adirondack Lake, New York State

# Heart Lesson

Lonely,
wandering,
stream-side pondering,
waves of "Why?"
and wiser ways of God.

Alone.

Looking past so many blessings
near at hand
I couldn't wouldn't understand
how God would ever love me.

Alone.

Rock-skipping promises,
suddenly I saw it there,
a perfect, heart-shaped stone.

The message God laid at my feet
was clear: "I am always here."

And grace set sail
my heart of stone.

Fall—Cicero, New York

# Hold On!

When the road is rough, full of twists and bends,
and you're tired and weary, and can't see the end,

Hold on!

When the dream you had seems tattered and gone,
you can't turn back and can't move on,

Hold on!

When all you held dear is left far behind
and all you seek you can't seem to find,

Hold on!

God knows your struggle, your heartache and pain,
the tears that you shed are never in vain.

Hold on!

God's grace is sufficient . . . he'll cause you to stand.
The Lord walks beside you and offers his hand.

Hold on!

Sunrise—Gulf of Mexico

# Holy Is Our God

Holy, holy, holy is our God.
Worthy, worthy, worthy is our King.

God Almighty, Jesus, his Son,
Holy Spirit. Three in one.

Alpha, Omega, beginning and end,
Jesus our Savior, redeemer, friend.

The heavens declare you, earth proclaims.
Oceans obey you, air breathes your name.

Grace so amazing flows from your throne,
truth unveiling, unto your own.

Love everlasting, mercy and grace.
Sweet Holy Spirit, come fill this place.

Holy, holy, holy is our God.
Worthy, worthy, worthy is our King.

Aurora, New York

# Joy Comes

I didn't know I needed him so much
until he was there, when he was needed,
in the pit of my despair.

Quietly, softly
he touched my life.

Gently, tenderly
he gazed into my eyes,
showing me a love so deep, so full,
my heart could not surmise the depth,
nor bear to look away.

He stayed.

In silence through the night,
absorbing tears.

In silence through the night,
erasing fears.

In silence through the night,
just being near
enough to touch, to see.

In silence through the night,
just for me.

Sinai desert near Jabil Musa

# Knowing You

Lord, I know you more
than I thought I ever could,
but my heart and soul
still long for more,
and all my life I would
so search your Word
and seek your face
'til all you find in me
is one desire—
to know you more
through all eternity.

Sight and Sound Millennium Theater—Lancaster, Pennsylvania

# Living Worship

Eternal Father,
Creator of everything,
I bring you my life
and I worship.

Most precious Savior,
Redeemer, coming King,
I cling to you for life
and I worship.

Holy Spirit,
Refiner of all I bring,
I sing through you for life
and I worship.

I bring all that I am,
cling for all that I'm worth,
sing through whatever comes
and I worship.

Rain forest—Costa Rica

# Love Came Down

Love came down in power
and penetrating light,
shattering the darkness,
turning back the night.

God came down.

Deep inside a flower
now begins to blossom,
forming in the likeness
of the brightest Son,

Christ in me.

In the final hour
Christ will come again,
revealing to all men
God's full sovereign plan.

Jesus, come.

He who began
a good work in the world,
he will complete his plan.

God never starts what he won't complete.
He will complete his plan.

Albino grasshopper—Mexico

# Meditation

Unlimited love,
forgive my limitations.

In external silence
and internal discipline,
give your peace from above.

Let all worldly thoughts
flow through, out, and beyond.

Give me your imagination.
Let your light shine within,
and let me know in contemplation
the pure mystery of you.

Aspen—Santé Fe, New Mexico

# Natural Cathedral

Leafy canopy
light and shadow panoply
God's covering of grace.

Glorieta Conference Center—Santa Fe, New Mexico

# New Song

Doubt conceals you, can't believe you.
Doubt would pass you by.

Fear can't face you, pulls away from you.
Fear won't even try.

Hope reveals you, longs to know you.
Hope trusts you hear my cry.

Faith believes you, stretches toward you.
Faith pushes past the lies.

God, you sought me, you reached down to me.
Your love draws me in.

Mercy sees me, dares to touch me.
Mercy heals the pain within.

Your grace turns me, your grace covers me.
Your grace cleanses all my sin.

Lord, I see you. I can hear you.
Your truth sets me free.

How I thank you, how I praise you.
I trust my heart to thee.

Lord, I love you, bow before you.
I give myself to thee.

Summit—Mount Sinai, Jabil Musa, Sinai desert

# Song of Ascent

Mountain air—
clean,
crisp,
clear.

Breath chatters
in the staccato shards
of an offbeat tune.

Too soon, I must rappel down
the granite face of life
to grapple with
more solid ground.

But I have seen the
glory and majesty
of my holy God
and I will rise again
to a song of ascent.

Gulf of Mexico

# Son-rise

In darkness
there is a light
invisible to human eye.

But claim it
deep within
your soul
and burning bright,
fed by love's
eternal flame,

Illuminate the night.

Rosamond Gifford Zoo, Syracuse, New York

# Thanks Giving

Father, thank you
for creation,
for snowflakes,
for morning drops of dew.

For a baby's cry
and a kitten's mew.

For diamonds in a grain of sand,
and wind-whispered, "I love you."

For things that surpass
our wildest imagination:
points of refracted light,
bound in radiant bows
thrown across the sky.

For hummingbirds, tripping light fantastic;
for bumblebees that don't know
they can't fly; yet they do.

But most of all,
for your amazing love
that shows how much you care
for all of your creation great and small.

Thank you.

Sunrise over the Atlantic Ocean

# The Glory of the Lord Has Risen

Arise, shine,
your Light has come
and the glory of the Son
flows from his throne
to fill his own.
Take the light and run!

Arise, shine,
like morning dawn
the rising of the sun
makes darkness light
dispels the night.
Take the light and run.

Arise, shine,
God knows that you
may be the only one
to bring the light
to one dark night.
Take the light and run.

White cranes—Rosamond Gifford Zoo, Syracuse, New York

# Unfathomable

God's patience . . . a virtue like no other!
He creates snowflakes, no two alike,
fills the universe with stars,
grinds tiny grains of sand.

Blends the colors of the rainbow,
draws the feathers of a bird,
fathoms the depths of the ocean
and forms a baby's hand.

Hand-molds a single human soul . . .
gives Jesus as our brother.

Costa Maya, Mexico

# Vessels of Clay

Imperfect clay
wedged between
heaven and earth,
patiently pressed
to remove
all impurity
that could weaken
the final vessel.

Molded, raised
by the Potter's hand,
fire-forged to hold
living water.

Perfectly designed,
intimately detailed,
signed and dated,
God-made pottery.

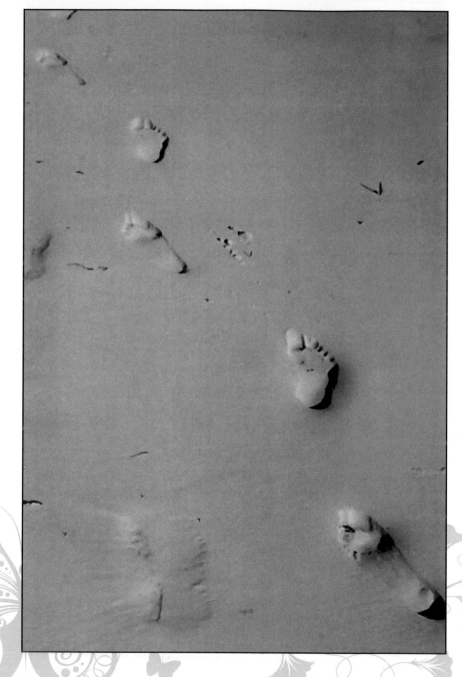

Beach—Princess Cay Island, Caribbean

# Will You Follow Me?

If I lead you far away
beyond what you can see,
past familiar here and now,

will you follow me?

If I lead you to the shore
and out into the sea,
upon the water, through a storm,

will you follow me?

If I lead you then to flames
and ask you to proceed
far into that fiery trial,

will you follow me?

If I lead you to a place
you'd rather never be,
place a cross upon your back,

will you follow me?

If I lead you just to take
one simple step of faith,
trusting me with all your heart,

will you follow me?

61